BBC TopGear

Where's Stig?

MOTORSPORT MADNESS

Illustrations by Rod Hunt

Words by Sam Philip

BBC BOOKS

CONTENTS

WHAT TO FIND ON EVERY PAGE

Jeremy

James

Richard

The Stig

P45

Richard's Africa
armchair

Bunga Bunga Stig

Stig's Credit Crunch
breakfast cereal

*170 National
Anthems* CD

Eels & Sodium
Delivery advert

Reliant Robin

James's pint of bitter

Richard's insect
repellent

Richard's baked
beans

Map of the source of
the Nile

Jeremy's
tennis racket

Jeremy's bicycle

Electric guitar

Boxing glove

Satellite phone

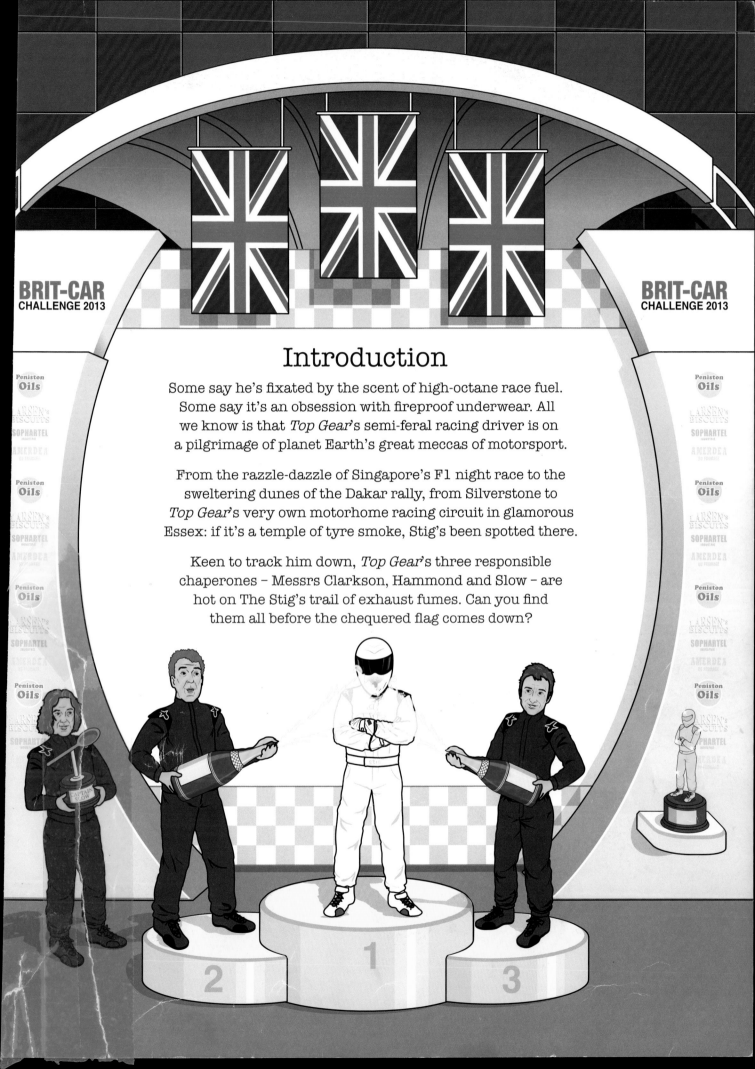

Introduction

Some say he's fixated by the scent of high-octane race fuel. Some say it's an obsession with fireproof underwear. All we know is that *Top Gear*'s semi-feral racing driver is on a pilgrimage of planet Earth's great meccas of motorsport.

From the razzle-dazzle of Singapore's F1 night race to the sweltering dunes of the Dakar rally, from Silverstone to *Top Gear*'s very own motorhome racing circuit in glamorous Essex: if it's a temple of tyre smoke, Stig's been spotted there.

Keen to track him down, *Top Gear*'s three responsible chaperones – Messrs Clarkson, Hammond and Slow – are hot on The Stig's trail of exhaust fumes. Can you find them all before the chequered flag comes down?

LE MANS

Welcome to the Circuit de la Sarthe, and the greatest endurance race on the planet. Twenty-four hours of blood, sweat and tears... and that's just for the poor soul tasked with finding our furtive foursome doing their best to ruin Audi's limelight-hogging dominance. Gentlemen, start your engines!

MOTORHOME RACING

No summer view cheers Hammond more than the sight of a convoy of motorhomes: provided, that is, they're going flat-out on a dusty motocross track and bashing fiberglass lumps from each other's flanks. Despite his well-documented allergy to Essex, Stig would never miss out on such wholesome family fun.

DAKAR RALLY

It's the world's most dangerous rally, a race so fiendish that it's not even held anywhere near Dakar itself. Though the cactus-strewn deserts of South America hold no fear for the creature known only in these parts as *El Stiggo*, can Hammond's beloved Wildcat survive the dunes? Or will it all end in Llamageddon?

LAS VEGAS DRAG RACE

The stakes are high on the Strip as *Top Gear*'s big rollers descend upon America's capital of vice. As usual, Stig's got his poker face on, but who would bet against the man who never, ever blinks first? And in the only city on earth that makes Jeremy seem quiet and understated, can the big man possibly get himself noticed?

ICELAND BUGGY RACING

It's all turned tectonic in the North Atlantic as an unpronounceable volcano spews more hot air than Clarkson stuck in a queue for a vegan burger bar. In a land of such murderous terrain and geological fury, no surprise that Stig has packed the beach towel and sunscreen for a relaxing island mini-break…

SINGAPORE

To Southeast Asia for the most glamorous night race on the F1 calendar, where cars stream below a million watts of dazzling artificial light, and shady millionaire team-owners order their drivers to crash. Enter three men who are quite capable of crashing without being told to.

ROMAN RALLY

In the beginning there was The Stig, and Stig said, 'Let there be racing!' And the racing was good. Friends, Romans and countrymen unite to hail the arrival of the Chosen One, but with their celestial sat nav ordering them to follow the star from the east, have our three wise men made it in time for the virgin birth?

NASCAR

Yee-haw! Welcome to the rootingest, tootingest heart of American motorsport, where the drivers are good ol' boys and the spectators are heavily armed. Hammond's right at home in Stetson country, but are those Secret Service agents simply looking out for Mr President, or closing in on the FBI's Most Wanted racing driver?

WALES RALLY

Bobble hats as far as the eye can see. All the mud you can eat. Tough to know why the Welsh rally doesn't inspire the same millionaire crowd as, say, the Monaco Grand Prix. Stig cares not for glitz or glamour, but with the locals' legendary penchant for mute, white creatures, he'd best keep on his guard.

INDIA HILL CLIMB

Holy cow! It's just not cricket as tuk-tuks battle elephants at the annual running of the *Top Gear* All Indian Classic British Hill Climb Event. High above Delhi's turban gridlock, a motley assortment of cars wheeze up the course, including every local's favorite: the Hindustan Ambassador. Or James May, as some know him...

BRITISH GP

The great and good of British motorsport have descended on Silverstone for the biggest date in the UK's racing calendar. Is this Stig's chance to settle the scores with Eddie Jordan after that nasty business with the ostrich and the Swedish beach-volleyball squad? And will that nice lady Jackie Stewart help May secure a podium finish?

TOP GEAR ULTIMATE TECH AND RESEARCH CENTRE

Here it is: an exclusive peek into the high-security birthplace of *Top Gear*'s most outlandish creations. It's a typical day in the office for *TG*'s crack team of hammer-wielding boffins, who are cooking up an F1 car and destroying an army of crash-test dummies. Or are those Stig's long-lost cousins?

CHECKLIST

YET MORE STUFF TO TRY AND FIND

LE MANS

- ❏ AF Corse Ferrari 458 Italia GT2
- ❏ Alarm Clock
- ❏ Aston Martin V8 Vantage GT2
- ❏ Audi R8
- ❏ Audi R15
- ❏ Audi R18
- ❏ Australian Flag
- ❏ Bentley Speed
- ❏ Canadian flag
- ❏ Corvette C6R
- ❏ Finnish flag
- ❏ Japanese flag
- ❏ Larsen's Biscuits sponsor sign
- ❏ Lola B08/60 Aston Martin
- ❏ Nissan DeltaWing
- ❏ Norwegian flag
- ❏ Pescarolo 01 Judd
- ❏ Peugeot 908
- ❏ Porsche 997 GT3-RSR
- ❏ Ten sleeping people
- ❏ *Top Gear* Britcar BMW 330D
- ❏ Toyota TS030 Hybrid
- ❏ Twelve grid girls
- ❏ Two Union Jacks
- ❏ Zytek Z11SN Nissan

MOTORHOME RACING

- ❏ Advert for Historic People Carrier Racing Championship
- ❏ Ambulance
- ❏ Chevrolet motorhome
- ❏ Citroen CX motorhome
- ❏ Classic VW camper van
- ❏ Essex lion
- ❏ Fiat Ducato MV70 Globetrotter
- ❏ Five squirrels
- ❏ Flatbed with caravan body on the back
- ❏ Ford Midas
- ❏ Land Rover 110 motorhome
- ❏ Lotus Excel motorhome
- ❏ Mitsubishi L3000
- ❏ Nine men in hi-visibility vests
- ❏ Old age people carrier
- ❏ Privy
- ❏ Raceway Tavern
- ❏ Range Rover

- ❏ SAAB camper van
- ❏ Six doves
- ❏ Teddy Bear
- ❏ Toyota Litace
- ❏ Tow truck
- ❏ Transit motorhome

DAKAR RALLY

- ❏ BMW X3
- ❏ Bowler Wildcat
- ❏ Car on fire
- ❏ Eight alpacas
- ❏ Eight lizards
- ❏ Hammer
- ❏ Hummer H3 buggy
- ❏ Iveco truck
- ❏ Kamaz 4911
- ❏ Mercedes Unimog
- ❏ Mini Cooper
- ❏ Mitsubishi Pajero
- ❏ Nissan Patrol Dakar
- ❏ Overturned motorbike
- ❏ Toyota Hilux
- ❏ TV news helicopter
- ❏ Two Argentinean flags
- ❏ Two Chilean flags
- ❏ Two Peruvian flags
- ❏ Volkswagen Touareg 3

LAS VEGAS DRAG RACE

- ❏ Aermacchi SF.260 plane
- ❏ Aston Martin Vanquish
- ❏ Bag of money
- ❏ Disheveled man
- ❏ Four white tigers
- ❏ Highway Patrol truck
- ❏ Lexus LFA
- ❏ Nine nuns
- ❏ Police car
- ❏ Sarcophagus
- ❏ Sheriff's truck
- ❏ Sphinx
- ❏ SRT Viper
- ❏ Ten piles of poker chips
- ❏ Thirteen Elvis Presleys
- ❏ Twelve Las Vegas cops
- ❏ Twenty-five showgirls

ICELANDIC BUGGY RACING

- ❏ Aquatic snowmobile
- ❏ Crane
- ❏ Erupting volcano
- ❏ Fifteen Icelandic flags
- ❏ Fire extinguisher
- ❏ Four Icelandic sheep
- ❏ Four Icelandic sheepdogs
- ❏ Fry-up
- ❏ Shovel
- ❏ Six Arctic foxes
- ❏ Toyota Hilux
- ❏ Twenty puffins
- ❏ Twenty-four molten fireballs
- ❏ Two reindeer

SINGAPORE

- ❏ Australian flag
- ❏ Brazilian flag
- ❏ Chinese dragon
- ❏ Dutch flag
- ❏ Finnish flag
- ❏ French flag
- ❏ Kung Fu fighter
- ❏ Mexican flag
- ❏ Singaporean flag
- ❏ Spanish flag
- ❏ Twelve police
- ❏ Twenty track marshals
- ❏ Two Finnish flags
- ❏ Two German flags
- ❏ Two Union Jacks
- ❏ Venezuelan flag

ROMAN RALLY

- ❏ Dead Roman legionnaire
- ❏ Eight camels
- ❏ Five goats
- ❏ Four men holding chickens
- ❏ Little Baby Stig
- ❏ Nine men riding motorcycles
- ❏ Six donkeys
- ❏ Thirteen Jordanian flags
- ❏ Thirty Roman centurions

NASCAR

- ❏ B52 bomber
- ❏ Barack Obama
- ❏ Cameron Diaz
- ❏ Chevrolet Camaro
- ❏ Eight Texan flags
- ❏ Four barbecues
- ❏ Four line dancers
- ❏ Jay Leno
- ❏ Jetpack man
- ❏ Man playing a banjo
- ❏ Man wearing 'Rock!' t-shirt
- ❏ Michelle Obama
- ❏ Parachutist
- ❏ Tom Cruise
- ❏ *Top Gear USA* presenters
- ❏ Two cowboys on horseback
- ❏ Winning driver firing guns

WALES RALLY

- ❏ Bentley Continental GT Speed
- ❏ BMW 328i
- ❏ Citroen DS3 WRC
- ❏ Ford Fiesta RS WRC
- ❏ Ford Escort Mk1
- ❏ Man with basket of leeks
- ❏ Mini John Cooper Works WRC
- ❏ Mitsubishi Lancer Evo X
- ❏ Nine Welsh flags
- ❏ Rocket man
- ❏ Skoda Fabia S2000
- ❏ Subaru Impreza
- ❏ Volkswagen Polo R

INDIA HILL CLIMB

- ❏ Austin Allegro
- ❏ Double bass
- ❏ Eight snake charmers
- ❏ Eighteen police
- ❏ Fifteen Bollywood dancers
- ❏ Five sacred cows
- ❏ Hindustan Ambassador
- ❏ Jaguar XJS
- ❏ Mahindra Thar
- ❏ Mini Cooper
- ❏ Rolls-Royce Silver Shadow

- ❏ Seven tuk-tuk taxis
- ❏ Tata Nano
- ❏ Three elephants
- ❏ Tractor and bowser
- ❏ Twelve Indian flags
- ❏ Two tigers
- ❏ Vespa

BRITISH GP

- ❏ Bernie Ecclestone
- ❏ Bulldog
- ❏ Chris Hemsworth
  (James Hunt in *Rush*)
- ❏ Christian Horner
- ❏ Damon Hill
- ❏ Daniel Brühl
  (Niki Lauda in *Rush*)
- ❏ David Coulthard
- ❏ Eddie Jordan
- ❏ Fernando Alonso
- ❏ Man wearing a kilt
- ❏ Mark Webber
- ❏ Martin Whitmarsh
- ❏ May's Quality Pies stall
- ❏ Mercedes SLS AMG
  safety car
- ❏ Murray Walker
- ❏ Nico Rosberg
- ❏ Nigel Mansell
- ❏ Ron Dennis
- ❏ Ron Howard
  (director of *Rush*)
- ❏ Ross Brawn
- ❏ Rubens Barrichello
- ❏ Sebastian Vettel
- ❏ Stefano Domenicali
- ❏ Sterling Moss
- ❏ Two Caterham cars
- ❏ Two Ferrari cars
- ❏ Two Force India cars
- ❏ Two Lotus cars
- ❏ Two Marussia cars
- ❏ Two McLaren cars
- ❏ Two Mercedes cars
- ❏ Two Red Bull cars
- ❏ Two Sauber cars
- ❏ Two Torro Rosso cars
- ❏ Two Williams cars

TOP GEAR ULTIMATE TECH AND RESEARCH CENTRE

- ❏ Aston Martin V8 Vantage
- ❏ Barbecue
- ❏ BMW Brutus
- ❏ Bowl of fruit
- ❏ Brian Johnson
- ❏ Bugatti Veyron
- ❏ Cessna 182
- ❏ Charles Dance
- ❏ David Haye
- ❏ Drum kit
- ❏ Eurofighter Typhoon
- ❏ Evolution of Stig exhibit
- ❏ Fighter Pilot
- ❏ Ford Focus ST Hatchback
- ❏ Ford GT
- ❏ Ford Transit van
- ❏ Gym
- ❏ HAL 9000
- ❏ Hover van
- ❏ Jackal armoured vehicle
- ❏ Jimmy Carr
- ❏ Joss Stone
- ❏ Kia C'eed
- ❏ London taxi
- ❏ Man on jet-propelled roller-skates
- ❏ Massage table
- ❏ McLaren MP4-12c
- ❏ Mike Rutherford
- ❏ Mitsubishi Evo
- ❏ Nitrous oxide Jaguar XJS
- ❏ Pink Stig
- ❏ Rachel Riley
- ❏ Radical SR3
- ❏ Ray Winstone and Ben Drew/Plan B
  (*The Sweeney*)
- ❏ Rubik's Cube
- ❏ Sabine Schmitz
- ❏ Simulator
- ❏ Skoda Yeti
- ❏ Stunt plane
- ❏ Ten boffins with hammers
- ❏ Ten car-body sculptors
- ❏ Vauxhall Astra Tech Line
- ❏ Violent Stig
- ❏ Warwick Davis

Rod Hunt would like to thank Derek Brazell and
Heng Khoo at The Association of Illustrators,
Matt Thomas at Mosquito Music, Matthew Wood at
Second Floor Studios & Arts, Russell Cobb,
Kim Vousden, *Top Gear* and Lorna Russell and
Joe Cottington at BBC Books.

Château Le Stig

2013

1 3 5 7 9 10 8 6 4 2

Published in 2013 by BBC Books, an imprint of Ebury Publishing.
A Random House Group Company.

Artwork © Rod Hunt 2013, Text © Woodlands Books Ltd 2013, Top Gear (word marks and logos)
is a trademark of the British Broadcasting Corporation and used under licence. Top Gear © 2005

The Random House Group Limited Reg. No. 954009

Addresses for companies within the Random House Group can be found at
www.randomhouse.co.uk

A CIP catalogue record for this book is available from the British Library.

ISBN: 978 1 849 90686 9

The Random House Group Limited supports the Forest Stewardship Council® (FSC®),
the leading international forest-certification organisation. Our books carrying the
FSC label are printed on FSC®-certified paper. FSC is the only forest-certification
scheme supported by the leading environmental organisations, including Greenpeace.
Our paper procurement policy can be found at www.randomhouse.co.uk/environment

MIX
Paper from
responsible sources
FSC® C013123

Commissioning editor: Lorna Russell
Project editor: Joe Cottington
Design: Two Associates
Production: Antony Heller
Printed and bound in Italy by Graphicom SRL
To buy books by your favourite authors and register for offers visit
www.randomhouse.co.uk